SOUTHEAST ALASKA

CLIFF & NANCY HOLLENBECK

PUBLISHED BY Todd Communications

ANCHORAGE, ALASKA

WITH OTHER OFFICES IN KETCHIKAN, JUNEAU, FAIRBANKS AND NOME, ALASKA.

SOUTHEAST ALASKA

Published by Todd Communications
611 E. 12th Ave.
Anchorage, Alaska 99501-4603 USA
Tel: (907)-274-TODD (8633)
FAX: 907-929-5550
sales@toddcom.com
WWW.ALASKABOOKSANDCALENDARS.COM

with other offices in Ketchikan, Juneau, Fairbanks and Nome, Alaska.

First printing April 2010
Library of Congress Control Number: 2009943947
Hard cover ISBN: 978-1-57833-480-3
Soft cover ISBN: 978-1-57833-477-3
Printed by Samhwa Printing Co., Ltd., Seoul, Korea
through **Alaska Print Brokers**.

All photography, text and design
© Cliff & Nancy Hollenbeck
cnimages@aol.com
www.hollenbeckproductions.com

Cover: Story of the Raven told by
Tlingit Herb Sheakley in Hoonah.
Previous page: Humpback whale breaches
off the coast of Southeast Alaska.
Left: Totem at Saxman Village, Ketchikan.
Back cover: Rafting on Mendenhall River,
McGinnis Mountain, left, and Bullard
Mountain, near Juneau.

WELCOME TO SOUTHEAST ALASKA

by Cliff & Nancy Hollenbeck

The look of Southeast Alaska, with its rich green rainforests dripping into the sea, towering rugged coastlines dotted with interesting towns, startlingly beautiful glaciers and majestic mountains, gives meaning to the word awe. Truly, this is a land worthy of a fearful and profound respect, a wonder inspired by greatness and grandeur. How can one see a mammoth glacier and not feel a sense of amazement, and also a little uneasy at the power of our natural world? These things alone are reason enough to visit this gorgeous area. Yet, there is so much more to Southeast Alaska.

The people who live and work along this rugged stretch of land and sea are a very special breed. They are tough and resilient, possessing a good sense of humor and a strong work ethic. This is not an environment for the pampered or lazy, but it is a place that attracts dreamers. Here the fruits of labor can be easily seen, the freedom longed for can be found, and the concept of community takes on a stronger meaning.

Johan Dybdahl, a Tlingit elder and historian at Icy Strait Point, told us a story of Jean Walsh, the former owner of Hoonah Cannery. She died in 1958 as a result of an earthquake in Southeast Alaska. Along with two friends, she was picking wild strawberries on a small island near Yakutat. When the earthquake occurred, an 1,800-foot wave hit the area and the island disappeared beneath 60 feet of water. This is just one story of thousands that is an example of the power of nature surrounding these communities and the strength of the individuals that call them home.

We traveled to Southeast Alaska to photograph the beauty of its natural surroundings and to showcase some of the amazing people who live and work in these communities. All of the people had interesting stories and every person was a pleasure to meet.

Rich Poor, and his wife Peggy, opened their hearts and home to us. Born and raised on the Douglas Island side of Juneau, Rich took us to the interview with State Senator Dennis Egan. They had gone to school together and partied as kids in the Governor's Mansion when Dennis's father was the first governor of the State of Alaska. He drove us to the newly opened ice rink dedicated in his father's name, Val Poor, and walked the shoreline of Douglas to give us good photo opportunities.

In Ketchikan we were invited to a Frank family Haida Clan celebration. The stage filled with about forty family members, ranging in age from a few months to the elderly. Their performances honored the senior Franks, "Mom & Dad," with legends told in music and dance. Beautifully hand sewn and decorated Haida robes moved across the stage and brought the ancient culture of a proud people to life. We were pleased to witness this celebration of family.

Andy Hoyt, a young father digging in the wet sand along Wrangell's Petroglyph Beach, told us about finding bottles that, in some cases, were over a hundred years old. "My daughters collect frosted sea glass, fill the bottles and sell them on ebay, under Alaska Sea Glass & Bottle," he said. "This stretch of beach was an old dump site, and everything from a fire on Wrangell's main street was dropped off a pier here in 1806. Some of what we have found is displayed at the Wrangell Museum."

Our Petersburg guide, Patti Norheim, is an 81 year old dynamo. We will never forget riding home with her one evening after a wonderful dinner. It was late and dark, and there wasn't another car on the road.

Suddenly she pulled over, stopped the car, opened her door and jumped out. As she began jumping up and down, she told us not to worry. It was a cramp in her leg. Almost immediately, a big pickup truck stopped and a young man got out. "Are you alright?" he asked with concern in his voice. "Oh, I'm ok," Patti said, still bouncing up and down. "What is your name? Who is your mother?" When the young man replied, Patti told him, "You're a good boy and I'll be calling your mother in the morning to tell her so." We know she made the call.

Brenda Schwartz's father, Skip, took us out to his smoke house five miles down the road from the main street in Wrangell, and gave us some of his delicious salmon. The next morning he drove to the airport to bring another bagful, as we waited for a flight. We ate on his generosity for the next few days. We received this same kind of bounty from the folks at Tracy's Crab Shack dockside in Juneau. They gave us extra crab legs and warmed us with their tasty crab bisque on a rainy Friday night.

We were especially touched by the many veterans throughout Southeast Alaska. Hoonah claims more veterans per capita than any other town in the United States. Along the streets we encountered parents of veterans, talked with older veterans and met amazing young men currently serving our country. "Wild Bill" Dalton was married the day before he drove us up the steep mountain road to the Icy Strait Point zipline platform. He is an active member of the National Guard and has twice been to Iraq. The priest at St. Michael's Russian Orthodox church in Sitka proudly says that he served in the Marine Corps. Brenda Schwartz and her husband were leaving Wrangell to attend the Coast Guard graduation ceremony of their daughter. There is a great sense of honor and patriotism among the people in all these small towns.

We were awed by the beauty of Southeast Alaska and honored to meet a few of her interesting citizens. This book is a glimpse through our eyes of its many wonders. We hope it will encourage you to visit and experience some of those same wonders. You will enjoy meeting "characters" in each city, seeing amazing wildlife and being stunned by the grandeur of the natural beauty. Southeast Alaska is an unforgettable experience.

We wish you Happy Travels,

Cliff & Nancy Hollenbeck

Frank Clan Haida Dancer S. Roger Alexander

Moss drips from a stately Western Hemlock tree. The majority of Southeast Alaska is part of the Tongass National Forest, which is part of the Pacific temperate rain forest. At seventeen million acres, about the size of the state of Maine, Tongass is the largest National Forest in the United States. Although populated by 75,000 people, much of the area is remote and home to rare plant life and a host of wildlife.

DENNIS EGAN
STATE SENATOR & RADIO PERSONALITY

"Southeast Alaska, the Panhandle of the greatest state, is a beautiful place. If you like the outdoors, you cannot beat this place. We are blessed with beautiful summers, like this year. It's unbelievable. Now we are surely going to have a real shitty winter. But we like the rain and shoveling snow. Believe me, I can use the exercise."

"The people here are fantastic. A lot of my friends and I disagree when it comes to politics, but when we are done discussing the issues we remain the best of friends. Some of my biggest supporters, when I was the mayor of Juneau, were people who opposed my positions. I am not talking just sort of against them, they hated my views. At the end of the day though, we got along and they voted for me or I couldn't have been elected. We remain best of friends to this day. We help each other shovel a driveway and help each other clean fish. It's a different environment. A different philosophy. It works for us."

"I am a relic of Southeast Alaska. I was born in Juneau, when Alaska was a territory of the United States. My dad represented the small town of Valdez in the legislature. I had a sister who was born there and she passed away. There wasn't a hospital, so my parents were very concerned and my mother came down to Juneau to birth me. She had me at St. Ann's Hospital, just a couple of blocks away from the capitol building. After I was born we went back home on the steamship Denali."

"The first eight years of my life we lived in Valdez. Every other year, back in the territorial days, the legislature would meet in Juneau. While my Dad was in session, I would go to daycare and kindergarten. He was elected to the Constitutional Convention, and then as a delegate to Congress as a (Tennessee plan) U.S. Senator. The family moved to Washington D.C. for a while. When we returned to Alaska he was elected Governor. That brought us to live permanently in Juneau. I fell in love with the city and never left. That was a long time ago."

"Juneau was small in those days. It still is today by most standards. You knew everyone. As kids we had the run of the town. The problem was everyone knew what trouble you got into, as well. You knew everyone's mother and father. It was no big deal that my father was governor. I was just one of the kids and raised hell like the rest of them. Probably too much hell. I even had a rock band that practiced in the Governor's Mansion. I think I spent a year or two on probation. I remember those days fondly."

"Our capital is small town Alaska. In fact, the whole state is the size of Bellingham, Washington people-wise. I don't care where you go in this state, you run into people you know. The state is still that small. But our land mass is about half the size of all the other states combined. The people in Anchorage, Fairbanks, Nome, Point Barrow and the Panhandle all have to understand each other's issues. Nothing is just a regional issue. Every event and every issue affects all of us. We're the only state government that provides gavel to gavel coverage of the legislature. The City and Borough of Juneau, plus the private sector, covers the entire cost to the tune of $275,000 a year. All so the citizens of Alaska can watch their government in action. That also makes Juneau a very giving community."

"I've learned a lot growing up with Juneau, and both of us have a few aches and pains to show for it. Even so, this is a wonderful part of Southeast Alaska, as I said, in the greatest of all states. The city of Juneau is a great place to live. My family is deeply rooted here. I will never move. Ever. My wife and I are here until we croak."

Hugging the steep, rocky, rainforest-covered hillside on the southwest corner of Revillagigedo Island, Ketchikan blends and flows along a picturesque coastline. While the city is several miles long, it is only a few blocks wide, with many buildings clinging to the solid rock slopes or hanging over the water on stilts. It's a dramatic natural setting for a city that shines like a necklace at the base of the land.

The fifth most populous city in Alaska with an estimated population of 15,000, it is named after Kitschk-hin, the Tlingit name for the creek that flows through the center of town. With an average annual rainfall that exceeds 150 inches, this is the wettest city in Alaska. In the winter there is an added snowfall of 37 inches.

Famous for its salmon, it was founded as a cannery and timber town. Commercial fishing still represents about thirty percent of the local economy. After the last of the timber industry closed in 1997, Ketchikan successfully pushed hard to make itself a major cruise ship destination. With several ships docking each day during the summer months, tourism has become the primary source of revenue.

Ketchikan has the world's largest collection of standing totem poles. Salmon bakes, performances at the Tlingit Native Saxman Village, float plane fishing trips, and watching bears fish for their own salmon are some of the interesting attractions that draw visitors.

Every summer Ketchikan's waterfront is a bustling scene of float planes, fishing boats, commercial barges, state ferries and cruise ships. Getting to the airport requires a trip through this water traffic on a small ferry. There isn't enough flat land for an airport on the city side, so it was built on neighboring Gravina Island. The locals still hope to build that "Bridge to Nowhere," which will connect Ketchikan to its airport and only source of flat land needed for commercial and residential growth.

Summer tourists and seasonal workers bring the revenue needed for locals to enjoy the peaceful, wet and cold days of winter. Then smaller groups celebrate relative isolation with bursts of artistic creativity, silly celebrations and private gatherings of friends and family.

Page 7: Thomas Basin Boat Harbor.
Left page: Tlingit totem face
  at Totem Bight Park.
Above: Great horned owl.
Right: Alaska State Ferry, *Malaspina*.

Above: Dolly's House on Creek Street. Brianna Krantz, dressed as Ketchikan's most famous madam, stands in the doorway.
Left: Boardwalk along Creek Street, once a famous red light district, now attracts tourists to gift shops and restaurants.

RAY TROLL
ARTIST & HIS 3D PAINTING

"This town is a funky, fun, unique place. There is nothing else like it in the world. I was glued here, by the good mix of an artist community and a tight circle of friends. My sister wanted to start a seafood retail store in 1983 and I came up to help. The seafood store isn't around, but I still am, along with a lot of my family. I'm an upstate New York guy that got stuck here in Ketchikan, Alaska."

"After six or seven years into it, I wanted to get the hell out of here. Good God, there is only 40 miles of road and I'd had enough. After all, I was an Air Force brat who had lived in eleven different places around the states and overseas. There had to be someplace I liked better than Ketchikan. I started looking around and found there is nothing else like it in the world."

"Ketchikan is truly a magical place. It inspires my work. It's a good mix of wilderness. I can head out the door and, in three blocks, be in the Tongass National Forest. Two blocks the other way is the ocean. When you look at most of my artwork, you see both the creatures in Ketchikan waters and the rainforest that surround us. The people in Ketchikan are also inspiring. It's not just the people who are here now, it's the deep culture that goes back ten thousand years. Where else do you get gigantic statues of powerful animals and strong figures? There are more totem poles here than anywhere else. This is an extraordinary place. Our population is fairly low, at about 13,000 now, we are down a thousand or so. I was here before there were stoplights, and now there are four. I was here before fast food and a mall. What's this town coming to? I'm getting to be an old timer."

"We raised two kids in Ketchikan. It's a wonderful place to raise children. They have a deep tie here. Conversely, I want them to go out and experience the world, too. One is going to college in California, while the other is in New York. Eventually, I could see them coming back here. There is something about Alaska that grows on you like a fungus, a mold deep in your pores. It is overwhelming when you leave here. Traffic, crowds, I can take it for awhile, then it is time to come back to Ketchikan."

Above: A ski plane flies over snow-covered Fish Mountain, just above the city of Ketchikan.
Left: Fishing boats ply the waters of Tongass Narrows.

13   Ketchikan Harbor along the Tongass Narrows, with Gravina Island beyond.

A colorful Tlingit button robe is worn by a Cape Fox performer at the
Saxman Native Village and Totem Park, just outside Ketchikan.

Above: Cape Fox dancer in traditional Tlingit dress.
Right: Clarita Seludo and her two month old baby
girl, Isabella, in ceremonial clothing.

15

WAYNE F. HEWSON
MASTER TLINGIT CARVER

"The Ketchikan area is such a cool place; it is a wonderful place to live. The Tongass National Forest is one of the last great rainforests in this hemisphere, with 17 million acres. You can't beat it. When you walk through the forest, or you are just sitting on the beach, or hanging in the mountains, being in nature feeds your soul. I would not trade it for anything."

"I was born and raised in Metlakatla, on Annette Island, just south of Ketchikan. I'm the fourth generation of my family to live in Metlakatla. There are only about 1,400 residents, but it is really a pretty place. Since we only live 14 miles apart, and go back and forth, Ketchikan is town and a second home for us. It is so close. We have friends and family in both towns."

"I am a Tlingit master carver. I apprenticed for ten years. Even when you are finished with your apprenticeship it is still an ongoing learning process, and I am still learning.

I work on my carving and talk to visitors here at the Alaska Rainforest Sanctuary during the summer. Now I have a son and two cousins that apprentice with me during the winter months. We teach classes on carving masks, bentwood boxes, bowls and other carvings…and that takes us through the winter."

"My home, Metlakatla, is just like my workplace, Ketchikan; they both share the same rainforests. It's such beautiful country. There is a yellow hill you can stand on and look out at the Pacific Ocean. Look north and you can see Ketchikan, and take a look up on Purple Mountain and see the profile of George Washington, a natural formation. It is really neat to see. I have two sons, David and Daniel, who love this land as much as I do, so there are more Hewson generations coming in Southeast Alaska."

16

Left page: Ravens are an important part of Alaska Native legends.
Above: Saxman Native Village and Totem Park.
Right: Alaska Rainforest Sanctuary walkway through Western
  hemlock and Sitka spruce trees.

Black bear with salmon catch.

WRANGELL

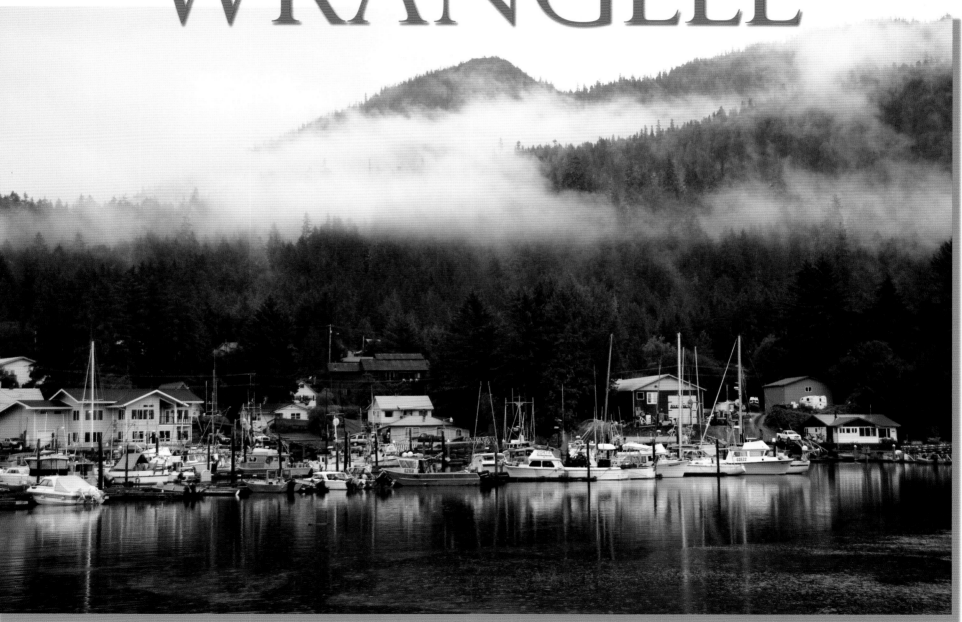

Originally a trading post for Tlingit natives and white settlers, Wrangell is the only town in Alaska to have been ruled at different times by four nations: Tlingit, Russia, Great Britain and the United States. Set in the middle of the Tongass National Forest, the small city is surrounded by a natural beauty of lush green rainforests, dramatic rocky shorelines, towering mountains, interesting beaches, 1,000 year-old petroglyphs and a beautiful harbor. The area is a scenic treasure.

Tlingits called the place Kaachxaana Akw. Fortunately for modern residents, it was renamed for Baron Ferdinand Petrovich Wrangell, the first head of the Russian interests in Russian America. He built a stockade near the clan house of Chief Shakes, which was later leased to the British Hudson's Bay Company and named Fort Stikine, after the local river. The area remained under British control, until Alaska's purchase by the United States in 1867.

With a population of 1,000 people, the town sits on the northern tip of thirty mile long Wrangell Island, and is the gateway to the Stikine River. Timber was the main source of income, but with that industry gone, commercial fishing and tourism sustain the economy. Wrangell shrimp are delicious and becoming famous as well. While big cruise ships rarely dock at Wrangell, smaller ships and independent travelers are discovering the untapped treasures of the surrounding wilderness and city.

The natural beauty blends with the town's outstanding museum and impressive Chief Shake's House, which dominates a tiny island just off the downtown shoreline in Reliance Harbor. It is a link to the Tlingit nation's past and a treasure of the present city. The Wrangell Weekly Sentinel was founded in 1902, and is the oldest continuously published newspaper in Alaska. Severe fires burned much of the downtown area in 1906 and again in 1952, destroying the historic buildings and changing the face of Wrangell into what it is today.

While the population in Wrangell has diminished in recent years, visitors are discovering its many interesting attractions, and tourism is beginning to grow. With strength, determination and independence, the people continue to survive and thrive as they have in the past.

Page 19: Homes along Reliance Harbor.
Left page: Bald Eagles are prolific in Alaska.
Above: Wrangell girl, Breanna Miethe.
Right: Street signs in Wrangell.
Far right: Kahlteen totem in Wrangell's
    Kiksetti Totem Park.

"Our people, the Tlingits, were settled down the channel a ways at a place called Old Town. The chiefs and warriors came up this way looking for a better place to live. First they stopped at Institute Beach, about five miles out the road. It has a creek that comes down. Then they found a bigger creek, called Mill Creek, that is across from the airport over on the other shore. They moved there because it was also at the mouth of the Stikine River. This area has a natural harbor. It has the protection of all the islands around it, so they decided to settle here. It was called Casa Clan. They traded with the sailing ships."

"I was born and raised in Wrangell, as were my parents and grandparents. I am one of the few elders who is truly from Wrangell. I was the youngest of eight. My parents passed away early. I came late in their life and my mother died when I graduated from high school. My father passed not long after. I have never lived outside of Wrangell. It's funny because when my husband passed away fifteen years ago, we were married about 50 years. I had a big house because I had five children. Then all the children grew up and moved and married. The first thing people asked was if I was leaving town. Why would I leave here? I did sell the big house to my youngest daughter and moved to a place five and a half miles out of town. It's right by a creek. It's beautiful."

"Since we don't get the big cruise ships here often, not much has changed

MARGE BYRD
TLINGIT ELDER

Left: Marge Byrd's niece
    Dawn Hutchinson-Stevens,
    at doorway of Chief Shakes
    Clan House.
Right page: Marge Byrd performs
    inside clan house.

in Wrangell over the years. Our timber mill closed and a lot of people left. The cannery wasn't running last summer and a lot more people left. That really hurt our school system. A lot of people moved up north, mostly to Wasilla. Now there are a lot of houses for sale and a lot of our businesses closed up. The cannery reopened this summer and that should help us. Most of our young people are fishing, because it pays well."

"The people are my favorite thing about Wrangell. For instance, night before last, one of our Wrangellites, a Chief Shakes descendant like myself, discovered he has cancer. So his family and his friends put on a great big benefit dinner, with a silent auction, to help him pay his medical expenses. They had a big turnout. Yesterday some friends put on a rummage sale to help a family whose husband had had an accident and is in rehab in Seattle. Then a young girl, who is going to college, she had gall stones and had no insurance, so they are doing a raffle to help with her medical expenses. We're like a big family here. Everyone in the whole community helps with what is needed."

"I try to visit my sister in Oregon, but I miss my mountains and my trees and my water so much that I can't stay away very long. Wrangell is home. It is a beautiful city and I would never live anywhere else."

BRENDA SCHWARTZ-YEAGER
ARTIST, CHARTER CAPTAIN, FIREMAN,
EMT & MOTHER OF FIVE

"Living in small town Wrangell is like a tapestry. You're connected to all these people. Your lives are all intertwined in some way. Your kids may go to school together; you go to church together, work together, or are on a volunteer committee together. We have all these ties. It is wonderful, because it makes the community as a whole strong."

"People often ask if I get bored living in a small town, or run out of things to do. Oh my gosh, there is a plethora of things to do at any given time, and I do lots of stuff. Some people dedicate themselves to one task. Not me. One minute I am stepping out of a boat after sharing this wonderful wilderness backyard I have with people from all over the world. Then I'll run into the studio and put finishing touches on a painting; at the same time one of my five children is asking what's for dinner that night. I am torn in a lot of different directions and sometimes want to say 'time out!' But I am never bored."

"Wrangell is a nurturing place. There is tremendous community support. People are esteemed for what they do and we are given a lot of opportunities. We have fabulous schools that are inspirational. I have never lived in a big city, and wonder if you would get lost in the shuffle. You don't in Wrangell. Here wonderful artists took me under their wings, loaned me paint brushes and encouraged me as a young kid. There are all these people who are pulling for you. If you are a kid here, and you show an interest in something, the whole community helps. People need and appreciate your talents and you can see the fruits of your labor. You do not blend into the masses here."

"I'm fourth generation Alaskan. I was born and raised in Wrangell. My Dad was born and raised here. I come from a commercial fishing family. While I have lived Outside and further north in Alaska, when it came time to start a family, I came home to Wrangell. A lot of kids grow up in Wrangell and feel it is very small and think they need to get out and see the world. Usually, not too long after they have seen some of the world, they decide Wrangell is a pretty exceptional place."

"We have a distinct sense of community. My nine year old son, Brian, can roam around the town while my husband and I are out on charters, and we don't worry. Everyone knows who he belongs to and watches after him. This is a village and everyone looks out for each other.

"Wrangell is being discovered by independent travelers. This is the place to come for the real deal in Alaska. It has what people think they will get when they visit. The stores on main street are owned by local people. You can go any direction outside of Wrangell in a boat and find some of the most incredible wildlife viewing opportunities in the whole state. Pristine, spectacular wilderness areas, incredible glaciers, bears and whales. All of the things people come here to see. We also have an amazing history, a strong artist community and an outstanding museum. This is a special place to live."

Left: Charles "Skip" McKibben, fisherman, salmon smoker and Brenda's father, at his smoke shack.

Above: Alaska Airlines jet makes approach
  to the airport near a wrecked ship at Petroglyph
  Beach State Historic Park.
Right: First discovered by the outside world in the
  1830's, more than 40 petroglyphs, thought to be
  thousands of years old, can be seen at Petroglyph
  Beach.

25

BRUCE HARDING
OWNER, ALASKAN SOURDOUGH LODGE

"Wrangell is a friendly community. Guests say it is like they have taken a step back in time. If they are walking along the road, locals will help them find something, or pick them up and take them somewhere. We have guests who arrive at the airport and locals will bring them in to the lodge."

"I moved to Wrangell in 1982. I had family here. At that time we were doing beach salvage, pulling logs off the beach. My Dad and my brothers had been up here since the middle 1970's. Then the opportunity to build the lodge came along, so my brother Todd and I helped my Dad build this place. Dad ran it for six years. Todd was doing charters on the Stikine River, trips to view the bears. I made my Dad an offer on this place he could not refuse and they got out. And here we are, it's twenty years later."

"I work with half a dozen independent tour operators. Most people come for the bears and salmon. The bears are a once-in-a-lifetime opportunity and can be seen April through August. June and July are when we have the king salmon runs and get most of our fishermen. The largest percentage of our visitors are from the West Coast of the U.S., although we also get some visitors from places like Australia, New Zealand, the U.K., Germany and Holland."

"This town has a great museum and we have the only USGA rated nine-hole golf course in Southeast Alaska. It has a corporate-sponsored tournament almost every weekend during the summer. We also have several interesting Tlingit Native celebrations at Chief Shakes Island, right in the middle of our harbor. Our Fourth of July celebrations are a big deal."

"I ask our guests why they picked Wrangell. Their overwhelming response is that it is the real Alaska. It's small town. The people are friendly and there's a lot of things to do. And Wrangell is a safe community. Very little crime. It's a tough place to make a living, but it's a great place to live."

Ancient eagle totem greets visitors to Chief Shakes Island and Clan House, which sits between Inner Harbor, left, and Reliance Harbor.

A float plane takes off from the waters along Zimovia Strait near Wrangell.

PETERSBURG

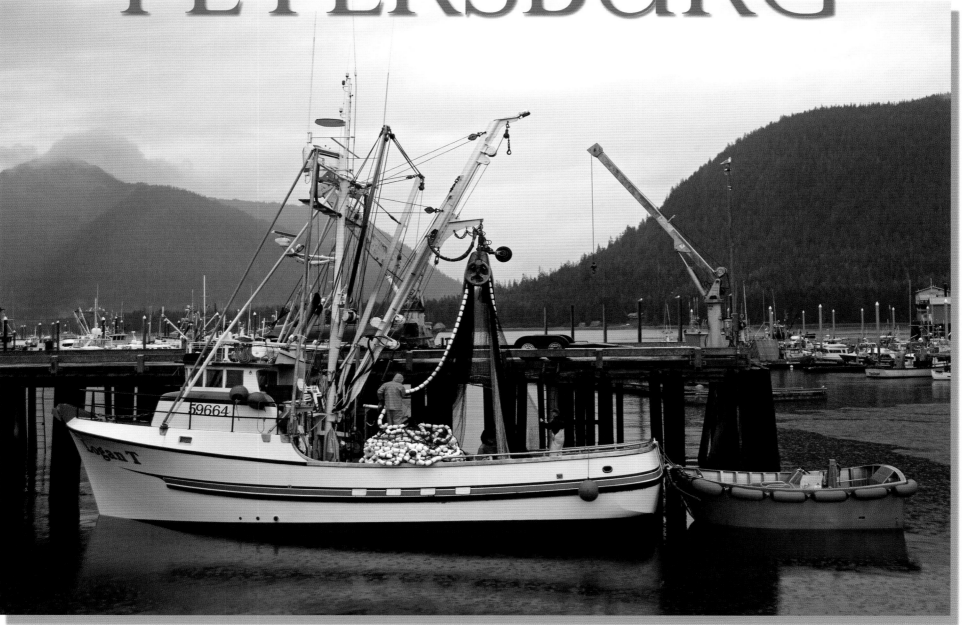

Norwegian Peter Buschmann sailed down the 22 mile Wrangell Narrows in 1897 and found, at the very northern end of Mitkof Island, a perfect harbor with abundant fish. He named the area Petersburg, after himself, built a cannery and convinced his friends in Norway to join him. Their descendants are still thriving in this vibrant community of more than 3,000 people.

Petersburg is surrounded by natural beauty. Rich green forests, towering mountains, abundant wildlife and teeming waters all combine to make the area picture-perfect. Home of the largest halibut fleet in Alaska, the town has four canneries and two cold storage plants, that process more than $32 million worth of seafood annually.

Nicknamed "Little Norway," Petersburg celebrates Norwegian Constitution Day the third weekend of every May. During those days locals dress, speak, eat, sing and dance in Norway's traditional manner. It is one of the most colorful and unique celebrations in the state.

Petersburg might seem to be a natural tourist haven. However, large cruise ships can't maneuver the 46 turns along Wrangell Narrows, so the city survives very well being one of the state's major fishing communities. Not being dependent on tourism has kept it more like a normal small town, the locals say. A small town in Norway.

Distinctive flowery Norwegian rosemaling art graces many of the local homes and businesses, adding to the quaint inviting look. Lawns are manicured, homes tidy, streets are clean and people are friendly.

The harbor is always busy with commercial activity. The town is a portrait of confidence and prosperity. The community cares about its environment, works hard to create a good life and, most of all, it is a place where people sincerely care about each other. Being a good neighbor is their lifestyle.

Page 29: The *Logan T*, owned by John Swanson, a seine boat at South Harbor.
Left page: Common seagull rests on a moss-covered piling.
Above: Planes moored at Petersburg Float Plane Dock, with seagulls and terns.

31

PATTI NORHEIM
CITY PIONEER
OWNER PATTI WAGON TOURS

"I have lived in Petersburg for 80 years. My whole life. There are two words that tell you what we have in this small town: people care. Everybody knows everybody. If anybody has a problem, everyone pitches in to help. Sally, my middle daughter, used to run away to the docks to find her father, who was a fisherman. I had a baby in the crib, so I couldn't leave to go get her. People along the way would take her in, give her cookies and call me to say she was there, having a good time, so I could come get her whenever I wanted. That was normal for our community, everybody watched out for everybody."

"Petersburg is so beautiful. We live on an island 25 miles long and 15 miles wide. There are more miles of road here than Ketchikan or Sitka, which are bigger towns. That's because we used to have a lot of logging here. Then logging kept getting smaller and smaller, and many families moved out. But the Forest Service was very good to us. They upgraded a lot of the logging roads and made them available to the public. One they upgraded is 21 miles long. It goes over two mountains and takes you to the end of the island."

"We are a fishing community. I would say 80 percent of the people are somehow connected with the fishing industry. There are many successful fishermen here who probably started on their father's boat and learned the trade. If they are really good fishermen, we call them highliners. We have a lot of highliners."

"My father came here in 1916 and started the first shrimp cannery. It was the only shrimp cannery in Southeast Alaska for many years. We ran the plant for 90 years. Now we do salmon, halibut, black cod, red snapper and we bring a five person team up from Japan that makes caviar from salmon. We no longer process shrimp."

"I was a cook on a shrimp boat when I was in middle school and my brother ran the boat. I did that for two summers. My Dad was a fish buyer. When he got a load of fish, maybe 50,000 pounds, the first thing they would do is cut the head off. The head holds the best part, it's called the halibut cheek and there are two on either side. I took orders from all the neighbors, for 25 cents a pound and would bicycle to the docks, stay there all day, cutting, washing and bagging halibut cheeks. With a basket on my bike and I would deliver them at night. I made enough money one summer to buy a portable radio for $90."

"Petersburg is a wonderful place to be. We have fish, we have trees, we have sunshine, and once in awhile we have a little rain. Quite a little rain. We have berries to pick, there are salmon creeks that people can fish in, there are trails, there are camping places for campers. One of them, the biggest one, is called Ohmer Campground, which is named after my father."

"I live on Wrangell Narrows, which separates our island, Mitkof Island, from Kupreanof Island across from us. Wrangell Narrows is 22 miles long, and is very twisty and turny so, the big tour ships can't navigate it. We are delighted about that. We would not want all those people coming here. It would create havoc. Petersburg is a thriving, close knit community and I hope it stays that way. It is the only place on earth I would want to live. And I love it."

Sons of Norway Hall, the center for Petersburg's culture, and the Valhalla, a replica Viking ship.

Shipyard Store sits on a pier along Wrangell Narrows, as a commercial seine fishing boat passes.

Above: Shalie Dahl sits in front of typical
Norwegian rosemaling folk art.
Right: Cynthia Benitz is dressed, like Shalie,
in traditional Bunad Norwegian attire.

JOHN & CAROL ENGE
CITY PIONEERS

"What do I love about Petersburg? My family started this town. It's my home. My grandparents were the first white couple to live in Petersburg. I was born here, grew up here, and have lived in Petersburg 94 years. Outside of attending the University of Washington and serving in the Navy during World War II, this has always been my home."

"I love the hunting and fishing and the freedom I have here. There is not much traffic. There is very little noise now. There was no noise when I grew up. You could hear a man fart across the bay. Pardon me. I could hear the birds. It was a good place to grow up."

"Both of my parents were from Norway. My grandfather came to Petersburg after his wife had died and then sent for my dad and his brother, John. My dad was fifteen and his brother was eighteen when they arrived. But John did not live long here. He went halibut fishing that first year and drowned. I'm named after him."

"My mother came in 1911, because her two brothers were in America. She stayed in Seattle for three years, working as a maid. She met my father there. He and her brother Ole were good friends. They were fishing partners at one time. My parents met, fell in love and got married in 1914. I was born in 1915, in Sing Lee Alley, in the Enge Building, in the southeast corner of the second floor. Several kids were born in that same room around that time. There was no hospital. I owned that building for several years and gave it to my sons. My oldest son lives on the second floor and my youngest son lives on the top floor. My middle son lives in Medford, Oregon. I have twelve grandchildren."

"I married a Petersburg school teacher on Christmas Eve, 1946. Carol was from Iowa. We didn't know each other very long, just from October to December. And hell, I was flat broke, didn't have a job. Later I managed canneries, cold storage, bought fish, I did everything in the fish business. I fished my way through college. I fished in the summer time. It took me six years to get through college, it was during the depression. Fished in the summer time and went to school in the winter time. I fished with my Dad and I was making good money. I had a car, joined a fraternity, I was doing okay. I fished for halibut, black cod, seine netted, and of course, gill netted. Had my own boat one year. I've done all kinds of fishing, except trolling. I have never trolled. I'm not a sport fisherman. I have only caught one fish in my life on a hook and line. One salmon."

"We raised five children in Petersburg, three boys and two girls, and it was a great place for them to grow. The town was smaller then and the children kept us involved in activities and we knew everyone in town. Now things have changed and we are less involved. When the kids are back in town, we hear about all the news through their friends. The young people go outside for work. Many come to work here in the summer. They miss this community when they are away. There is no traffic. That's the best part of Petersburg. And the freedom you find here. It's home."

Above: The *M/V Spirit* owned by Ronn Buschmann in Petersburg's Middle Harbor.
Below: Commercial fisherman sorts salmon catch.
Right: Nick Gilbert processes coho salmon at Tonka Seafoods plant.

Black bear fishing for salmon near Mendenhall Glacier.

JUNEAU

No roads lead to Juneau. It's the only mainland state capital that can be reached only by air or sea. Add ice fields the size of Rhode Island and you have a very special city. The area of the City and Borough of Juneau is the size of Rhode Island and Delaware combined. It's the third largest municipality in the United States, eclipsed only by Yakutat and Sitka. Despite this size, the population is about 30,000, making it one of the smallest capitals in population.

Mendenhall Glacier, just north of downtown, is the most accessible glacier in Alaska. The icebergs, black bears and raft trips found at Mendenhall Lake, at the base of the glacier, come as a stark contrast to nearby government offices. The city center hugs Mt. Juneau and Mt. Roberts, while looking across Gastineau Channel at the towering peaks of Douglas Island. The channel is alive with cruise ships, float-planes, barges, ferries, smaller tour boats and fishing boats during the summer. Tourism dominates the summers and politics dominates the winters.

Juneau was founded as a gold rush town. In 1880 Joe Juneau and Richard Harris discovered gold in the creek that runs through downtown. It became known as Gold Creek, igniting a gold rush to Alaska. Gold in local streams was quickly exhausted and underground mining began. The flat area of land that became the downtown is built on tailings, the crushed rock discarded along the shoreline after the gold was removed. The gold rush created Juneau and made it the economic center of Alaska. The legislative capital was moved from Sitka to Juneau in 1906.

There is still mining in Juneau, but on a much smaller scale. It's government and tourism that make the city come alive. More than 500,000 cruise ship passengers visit each year, but it's the strongly independent residents weathering the harsh winters who make Juneau thrive.

Juneau has the largest population in Southeast Alaska, but it still holds on to Alaskan small town values. Hiking trails lead out into the wilderness from many back doors. This city has one foot in the modern world of international government and the other in the legends of a last frontier. It's a challenging and exciting mix that makes Juneau a great city.

Page 39: Mendenhall Glacier above Auke Bay,
  Mts. McGinnis and Stroller White at left.
Left page: Dog sledding on Mendenhall Glacier.
Above: TEMSCO helicopter lands on Mendenhall Glacier.
Right: Mt. Roberts Tramway above Gastineau Channel,
  downtown Juneau and bridge to Douglas Island.

RIE MUÑOZ
ARTIST OF ALASKA NATIVE LIFE

"I came up to Juneau on a tour boat. It was a beautiful sunny day on the first of June 1950. The city was gorgeous as the ship was landing. While we were still tying up to the dock, I decided to see if I could find a job here. The boat was traveling on to Skagway and then back to Juneau. If I could find a job and a place to live, when the boat came back I would take my suitcase off and stay."

"The first place I tried was the Alaska Sunday Press. I got a job. I wanted to live in a nice neighborhood, and the neighborhood up the hill was very nice. There was a woman hanging up her laundry and I asked if there were any rooms for rent and she had one. It wasn't really a rental room. It was a big closet with a bed in it that went from one wall to another. She rented it to me for five dollars a week. She weighed about 300 pounds and loved to cook, and she always invited me for dinner. She was a great character."

"I was totally intrigued by Alaska. After living in Van Nuys, outside Los Angeles, and working at a department store decorating windows, Alaska was so much more interesting. California was really boring and had all that smog. I couldn't find many things that interested me to paint. I was really happy to get out, although my family didn't think it was a great idea to stay in Alaska. It was during the cold war and Alaska was close to Russia."

"I married a Philadelphian in Juneau. He was a geologist and wanted to prospect. For prospecting you needed a grubstake. We figured where could we possibly go for jobs, to get a grubstake, and thought teaching out in the bush would do it. That was our aim. So we went to see Hugh Wade, head of the BIA (Bureau of Indian Affairs) at the time, and asked if there were any teaching jobs available. He said there was one on King Island and another at Sleetmute on the Kuskokwim River. We had never heard of King Island or Sleetmute, so we went straight to the library and checked them out. King Island was really isolated and very primitive, so we chose it. My parents didn't like it at all. The kids didn't even speak English, so that made it difficult. We earned our grubstake and went out prospecting. We loved our whole experience on King Island."

"In 1972 I quit working and started painting full time. I am really fascinated with the different kinds of work people do. I don't paint for the beauty of things. I like painting every day things. Some of my paintings are totally imaginary, like the one of the scary sea. I was inspired by that one when I lived on King Island. I would see the Eskimos digging big holes in the ice, the ocean below was pitch black and they would just pull up anything that came by. I thought, God, what is underneath there? So I drew that picture of what I thought was under the sea. I like to draw Eskimo legends too. That's because you can make up anything you want to, more or less, exaggerate things."

"My parents came up to visit me in Alaska. They loved Juneau. I think anyone who comes up from the lower states loves Alaska. All the people visiting on tour boats, I imagine that they all love Alaska. I love the Alaskan people. I love to paint people. The more population the worse people behave. Here there are not so many people. Alaska is so special. We are around all this fantastic nature, the whales breaching, bears in your backyard and moose wandering around. Life here is so interesting."

Float plane on Auke Lake with McGinnis Mountain in background.

Left: Glacier Gardens Rainforest Adventure guide Kylie King.
Above: Tracy LaBarge, owner of Tracy's King Crab Shack.
Below: Arlene Tripp at Mt. Juneau Trading Post.

44

GEOFFREY AND MARCY LARSON
OWNERS, ALASKAN BREWING COMPANY

"After five years of living in Alaska, we could tell stories about the wildlife and the beauty, but it was the people who made us so committed to Juneau. To Alaska. It was the people who supported our dream to start a brewery."

"I came for a summer job in Glacier Bay National Park," Marcy Larson continues, "fell in love with Alaska and never left. Geoffrey followed after we met and fell in love in Montana. In 1980 we moved to Gustavus and knew we wanted to live in Alaska. Geoffrey is a chemical engineer and I'm an accounting person. It was really tough to make a living in a town of only 90 people."

"We moved to Juneau where I worked for the state and he worked at a gold mine. Both of us tend to work really hard, and noticed we were spending a lot of time working, but weren't working together. So when the gold mine went under, we decided to do something where we could work together and make a living in Alaska."

"At that time Geoffrey was home brewing. It started as a joke, when a friend suggested starting a brewery. That little tidbit got us looking into it. One thing lead to another and we started the process of raising money. While the banks were gracious, they all said no. Back in the late 1980's it was a tough time. There were a lot of foreclosures at the time. Our families said no too. They all said it nicely."

"Looking at it objectively, my goodness, why would you invest with us?" Geoffrey remarked. "I had only been here two years; Marcy had been here for three. We're in our mid-twenties. What a crazy idea, starting a brewery in Juneau. It took us a full year to raise the money. It was small town Alaska that made our brewery. We raised money from Ketchikan to Kotzebue. We were everywhere in Alaska, big and small communities. The only requirement was that investors had to be Alaskan. We had people who were loggers, miners, park service employees, attorneys and accountants. Many of them didn't see eye-to-eye, but the one thing they agreed on was beer. Small town Alaska came through for us."

"It got down to the last day of our deadline. We had maxed credit cards, called everyone we could think of and were down to the wire. At our final escrow meeting, we were going over the documents with three people who were going to pool their money to buy the last share. We did all the signing and it was time for the checks. One of the people didn't have enough money in her checking account and wanted to do it the next day. The bank closed at 4:30 and it was 4:15. If we didn't have the money that day, the escrow company would send it all back. The woman was allowed to write one check a month on her savings, so she wrote that check. We walked in to the title insurance company at 4:25 pm."

"In 1986 we sold our first bottle of beer. We started out just selling locally. We bottled first, before it was kegged, which is backwards from other breweries. There wasn't much of a draft market up here at that time and we had to bring the kegs up and then ship the kegs back down. Our first beer was called Chinook Alaskan Beer. The original sign is still in the warehouse."

"Juneau is a great place to do business, especially for a young, upcoming, no experience couple who are just looking to make a living. We had no experience, no money, no roots, no equity and the people of Alaska invested in us. All because we love beer and are passionate about what we do. We wanted to live in a city and state that we loved, and we do… Juneau, Alaska."

Left: St. Nicholas Russian Orthodox Church.
Right: Cross at the Shrine of St. Therese.
Below: Old saltwater pump house, part of Treadwell Mine
  ruins on Douglas Island. Juneau harbor in background.
Right page: Mendenhall Glacier flows into
  Mendenhall Lake.

Cruise lines, like Holland America, dock at the Juneau pier and bring about 500,000 tourists to the state capital each summer.

HOONAH

Hoonah has been called "The Little City with a Big Heart." Located 50 miles west of Juneau at the northern end of Chichagof Island, it is the largest Tlingit village in Alaska. Over 70 percent of the 850 residents are of Alaska Native heritage. The town sits within the Tongass National Forest, which is about the size of Indiana, making it the largest national forest in the United States. It was named after the Tongass clan of Tlingit people. The small town's natural setting is beautiful. The nearby forests of Chichagof Island are home to the largest brown bear population in the world, averaging three bears per square mile.

While primarily a fishing community (over 100 residents hold commercial fishing permits) Hoonah is quickly becoming a popular tourist destination. One of the world's most productive salmon canneries was built just down the road in 1912. Long after it closed the Huna Totem Corporation purchased the cannery and, after extensive renovations, it has become a unique and exciting cruise ship destination called Icy Strait Point.

Today visitors explore the cannery museum and shops, enjoy native legend shows, go on wildlife tours, or have the thrill of a lifetime on the world's longest zip-line. There are bus tours around the Hoonah area, which is home to most Icy Strait Point workers. Since the Tlingit people own and operate this tourist destination cannery, visitors are warmly welcomed in the small community.

Residents take great pride in their town, Native culture, close-knit families and especially their military veterans. Per capita, this small town claims more veterans than any city in the United States. They are proud Tlingit warriors, who have earned the respect of their country.

Page 49: Downtown faces Hoonah Harbor
   along Port Frederick waterway.
Left page: Humpback whale breaches in Icy Strait waters.
Above: St. Nicholas Russian Orthodox Church.
Right: Hoonah tour bus travels Cut-Through Road between
   Icy Strait Point and the village.

HERB SHEAKLEY
TLINGIT CLAN HISTORIAN

"My Tlingit name is Yun Dus. I am a Thunderbird on my mother's side. My father comes from the Raven of the Snail House in Hoonah. I am a grandchild of the Chookaansha Eagle Bear."

"My family has been in Hoonah for five generations. It is in our hearts and souls. I love the history; it tells me about my people. How they survived together. How the different clans became as one and held each other up, whether you're a Raven or a Thunderbird. This is a big part of how this community stands tall. Standing up for each other, sharing our cultural pride in our songs and stories, that is how we show our pride. That is how Hoonah stands tall."

"Hoonah is right in the middle of the Tlingit Nation. It runs from Ketchikan to Yakutat. We are on islands all over Southeast Alaska. Hoonah means "Protected from the North Wind." There is a lot of pride in being part of the Tlingit culture. We are building on that pride. When I was growing up I did not know or understand my own culture. After the year 2000 I really began to study it."

"When we talk about our stories we go and talk to the elders. Always getting permission from them before we do anything within the boundaries of our culture. We need their okay. To show respect is what we are trying to do. We hope the younger generation will do this also because they are there for us to pass down our culture. We have to ask the questions and now the elders are answering us, which is really nice."

"The way the Tlingit people first came here from Glacier Bay is a story we tell which dates back 12,000 years. Five clans lived in Glacier Bay for hundreds of years. Up into the Fairweather Mountains, where they lived with the bears. Then finally the glacier was breaking apart and moving, at that time it was crushing the clan people. A lady there, because she had seen her people already covered by it, asked the surviving people to leave the glacier. All the other clans got in their canoes and they left. My people came around from Glacier Bay and settled on the Point, when Hoonah was basically ice country because of the glacier. But they lived there."

"I have been working with my mother getting the family stories together. I made a staff for her. It tells the story of her people. She was telling me about it and, like myself, she had nothing to show for who they were. We talked about it and I started picturing what I wanted to carve on the staff. Stories are told beginning at the bottom of the staff."

"I did a staff for my girlfriend Betty Ann. It shows her brothers; one that passed on is represented by the spirit of the eagle. A beaver at the top represents her dad's tribe overlooking the family. This summer she picked up a rock and tossed it into the water. About two minutes later, a beaver was swimming there and he came and dove down where she threw the rock. She stood by the water and the beaver came and put the rock down by her foot. I said, 'See your dad came to say hi to you.'"

"Hoonah is a place of many Tlingit legends. I try to tell my people's stories through carvings, songs and dance. That way they will be carried on in the minds of our children."

Herb Sheakley home.

The village of Hoonah, along the waters of Port Frederick, from a Wings of Alaska flight.

Left: Pier stretches into Hoonah Harbor.
Top: Forest above Hoonah, part of Tongass National Forest.
Above: Devil's club is common in rain forests and used as
    food and medicine by Tlingit Natives.

Above: Icy Strait Point cannery buildings and docks,
where the waters of Icy Strait and Port Frederick meet.
Right: Tlingit dancer Cristina Contreras in traditional dress.

55

JOHAN DYBDAHL
ICY STRAIT POINT TLINGIT ELDER

"In 1947 when I was two months old, my family moved into a cottage at the Hoonah Cannery, which is now part of Icy Strait Point. We lived there year 'round, my parents and the four of us kids. At that time the road to town was not maintained in the wintertime, so we had to go from here to Hoonah by skiff to attend school. That became a little onerous after awhile, so my Dad bought a little house in Hoonah. We moved there in 1955."

"When I was growing up, I knew everyone in Hoonah. They say it takes a village to raise a child and the people here acted like that towards me. There was an airplane float right down there in the water. I fell off of it one time and my brother Paul saved me with a purse seine plunger. I had fallen overboard two or three other times. Some old ladies came to see my mother after I had been rescued asking her for my clothes and my shoes. They took them down to the shore and put them on a stump, where the tide would wash them away. They believed the sea spirits were after me and now they would believe they got me."

"I started commercial fishing by myself when I was eleven years old. I had friends that would watch me come and go. If I was late returning, they would come down and ask my mother where I was and why I wasn't back yet. People look out for each other in Hoonah."

"There were about 600 people in Hoonah when I was growing up. There are about 875 now. We are the only village that is growing in Southeast Alaska. It makes me sad to think many others are losing their population. They have no economy. Tourism has been good for our people."

"Icy Strait Point is a family operation... from the time it was Hoonah Cannery to now. Recently I was digging in a sand box my dad built and found a little molded plastic Indian. I remember when I was six years old the only way we could get things was from the Sears and Roebuck catalog. I wanted this Fort Apache set and, low and behold, Santa Claus brought it. Now I found one of the toy Indians 55 years later.

"When we put the Icy Strait Point project together, we felt that many visitors were not getting a taste of the real Alaska. So we formulated three main themes for our project. One is based on the local native culture. We are the largest Tlingit village in Southeast Alaska. Second, we highlight the history of the cannery. And last, we showcase the abundant wildlife. We also acted as our own general contractor so all the things you see here are built by the people who own it. The people were bought into the project in a very big way and it makes them more proud of what they are giving. We have no vandalism, no problems like that, because this project was built by the people. We have a beautiful location, great facilities and best of all we have wonderful people here at Icy Strait Point. They are our best asset."

Lauren, left, and Erin Gaffaney sit in harnesses ready to ride the Icy Strait Point zip-line. This is the world's longest zip-line at 5,330 feet, dropping 1,300 feet at speeds up to 60 mph.

A U.S. Coast Guard helicopter flies above the icy face of Margerie Glacer in Glacier Bay National Park and Preserve.

GLACIER BAY

Glacier Bay is stunning. This majestic iceberg-filled bay has several inlets flowing into it, along with towering moving glaciers. There are mountain peaks in every direction adding their grandeur to the backdrop. Icebergs in various shades of blue and in all sizes float toward the open water. The enormous glaciers descending from the high snow-capped mountains, cutting through land, pushing into the inlets and dropping icebergs to float away are awesome in their size and power. The scene is so grand, so unforgettably amazing, that everyone should try to see it in their lifetime.

The first written mention of the Glacier Bay area was made by Captain George Vancouver in 1794. At that time the bay was solid ice and was only a brief passage in his journals. The Tlingit Natives, who by Vancouver's time were living in nearby Hoonah, had long lived and hunted in the Glacier Bay area.

It was John Muir's legendary trip into Glacier Bay in 1879 and his impressive descriptions that brought the world's attention. The noted naturist left Wrangell in a canoe with three native paddlers and a missionary friend to explore the area. Just navigating the powerful and dangerous waters in such a craft was a major feat of bravery. To paddle into Glacier Bay and discover the wonders of its eleven tidewater glaciers,

one of which now bears his name, was nothing short of a miracle. His journey and well-circulated writings resulted in Glacier Bay becoming one of the major tourist sites in the Western Hemisphere. The area was named a U.S. National Monument in 1925 and then re-designated Glacier Bay National Park and Preserve in 1980. The 5,130 square mile area is included in an International Biosphere Reserve and is part of a UNESCO World Heritage Site. There are now nine tidewater glaciers, four of which actively calve icebergs into the bay. No roads lead to the park and it can only be reached by air and sea. Despite the lack of roads, more than 300,000 visitors enjoy the area each year. Most arrive via cruise ships.

The bay is home to a variety of marine life. Sea otters, porpoises, sleek killer whales, harbor seals and powerful, gigantic humpback whales. There are also wolves, moose, mountain goats, a wide variety of birds and both brown and black bears. These creatures gave life to the original Tlingit clans.

Glacier Bay is a highlight of any Southeast Alaska trip. Its spectacular scenery is unforgettable. It provides a glimpse at the amazing natural phenomenon of living glaciers, and a new appreciation for the power and beauty of our natural world. It's an experience not to be missed.

Page 59: Cruise ship glides through the
calm waters of Glacier Bay.
Page 60: Margerie Glacier is 21 miles long, beginning
at the south slope of Mount Root in the Fairweather
Mountain Range.
Above: Cave in the face of Margerie Glacier.
Right: Sun reflects on Glacier Bay waters.

Left page: Gilkey Glacier, west of Glacier Bay, flows
through the Coast Mountains.
Above: Holland America Line's *MS Volendam* in front of
Margerie Glacier.
Right: Tourist photographs from cruise ship railing while
traveling in Glacier Bay.

Sitka Roses in bloom.

SITKA

Sitka is arguably the prettiest city in Southeast Alaska. It also has a rich and colorful history. Originally the Tlingit natives gave the town its name, which means "In This Place." When Russians settled the area in 1799, they called it Novoarkhangelsk, or New Archangel, after the home town of the first governor Alexander Baranov. Though the Tlingits fought Russian settlement, it became the busiest port on the west coast of North America and capital of Russian Alaska. Everyone, even the Russians, continued to call it by the Tlingit name Sitka, as they do today.

The Russians slaughtered the sea otters for their fur trade almost to extinction and Sitka, as well as all the Russian holdings in Alaska, were thought to be worthless. When the United States purchased Alaska from the Russians in 1867, the formal transfer ceremonies took place here. After the Russians left, the town became the first capital of Alaska, but following the turn of the century the seat of government moved to Juneau.

Sitka became a quiet logging and fishing port community. There was an influx of U.S. Navy personnel when the Japanese invaded the Aleutian Islands during World War II. The small town returned to timber and fishing following the war. When the timber mill closed in 1993 this small town of 9,000 people turned to tourism and the arts. It was a natural transition, with more than twenty buildings and sites in the National Register of Historic Places.

Sitka sits along the ocean on the west side of Baranof Island. It looks out at dozens of tiny forested islands nestled along a gorgeous coastline. The surrounding scenic beauty is matched by the picturesque town. The Russian past is a major attraction for visitors from around the world, symbolized by the town's beloved St. Michael's Russian Orthodox Cathedral in the heart of the city. Tlingit, Russian and American cultures combine with wildlife, the arts and scenic beauty, to make this gem of a city.

Page 65: Sitka Channel, city and Mt. Verstovia.
Left page: New Archangel Dancer Linda Speerstra
  performing Russian folk dance.
Above: Russian Orthodox Priest Rev. Fr. Elia Larson.
Right: St. Michael's the Archangel Cathedral.

TOMMY JOSEPH
TLINGIT CARVER

"Sitka has amazing natural beauty. The mountains are gorgeous and the open ocean is right in front of us. There are so many places to go in a boat. There are trails to hike all over these big mountains. The fishing is amazing. You can kayak. There is just so much to do around Sitka. The setting here is so beautiful."

"Twenty five years ago I came to Sitka for a visit in the winter as it was just going into spring... stayed for almost a month and decided this was the place for me. I went home to Ketchikan, packed my bag and moved here. Sitka is beautiful, clean, quiet, clear air all the time. Fresh air is all over Southeast Alaska. I just really like it here. It's my hometown now."

"Sitka is smaller than Ketchikan, and quieter. Ketchikan was a great place to grow up, but it has gotten more into tourism and that changes a town. Sitka hasn't done that. This town is so into the arts, with a lot of community functions and events that happen. There is always something to do here."

"There is a thriving culture in Sitka, the people are so active. There is a lot happening here. There is a good mix of people. I didn't know much about the Russian culture before I moved here. Even though I grew up only 200 miles down the coast, I had never even heard of the Russian Orthodox Church until I moved to Sitka. It's a big part of the community because of all the Russian history in this town. I have learned a lot about their influence here. I just returned from a visit to St. Petersburg in Russia. They have a huge collection of our artifacts in a museum there which they took from Sitka when they left. So I went over and paid it a visit. I was on a world tour of museum collections. I got to visit 19 different museum collections in eleven weeks. It was amazing."

"Seeing incredible art around the world has inspired my art here in Alaska. I started carving when I was eight, in the third grade. That is when I got my first exposure, to really hold a knife and do some carving. Sitka has helped nurture my art. The people, the setting, the community have all given me opportunities to grow in my art. It's a great place to live."

Above: Sitka Pioneer Home and the Prospector Statue.
Right: Totem at Sitka National Historical Park.

TERI ROFKAR
TLINGIT WEAVER

"My Tlingti name is Chas'Koowu Tla'a. I am a Raven from the Snail House. We are weavers in our family, that is what we do. I was born in California. My dad is not Native; my mom is Tlingit. I have family here in Sitka. It is a great place to raise a family. I have three children and they are all grown. My granddaughter spins and weaves, so I am passing along our ancestors' art form."

"I have lived in Sitka since 1976. My grandmother was born here in the 1800s. My mother went to school here. Sheldon Jackson was a boarding school for Native kids. The Native kids were not allowed to go to public school until the riots in the early 1960s."

"While I am striving to recapture the woven arts of my ancestors, weaving is a dying art. I can go to a museum and get paid for a book about the weaving I do. I can get compensated for demonstrating. But they are not purchasing. I am working with a museum back East, working on a book, because they have 500 Tlingit baskets. The last time they bought a basket was 1932. How can our young people survive making baskets? Even the Smithsonian does not have one of these geometric robes. They are in St. Petersburg, Russia, they are in other communities, but they are not here. It has to change if we are going to keep weaving alive. At a textile museum they say with urgency that they are in Burma to preserve fragile art forms before they die. I ask, have you seen what is in your own backyard?"

"Our art preserves a part of our ancestor's weaving skills. It displays the intimate relationship with place that our objects represent. Using mountain goat wool for example. And these objects will last two to three hundred years, even under heavy use. But that is not of value in today's world. Even the Native corporations are for profit. Their job is to cut down the timber and sell it to Japan and make a profit. They are not humanitarian or social groups, they are for profit. They are trying, but it isn't their focus. It isn't the mandate of the Native land claims federal bylaws."

"The young people in our community cannot afford to carry on our art forms. They desperately want to, but I hardly make over minimum wage and I am at the top of my game. So I am sad about our ancestor's art forms."

"I continue to do my work with respect for my past and appreciation for my environment. Sitka has a lot of artists. Part of that is the isolation. We don't have the distractions of everyplace else. These projects take a lot of time. This robe I am weaving will be a year and a half of my life put into one piece. I weave full time."

"We found a basket that is 5,000 years old. The roots are split exactly the same way I do it today. The weaving is the same. That is what I taught my daughter and now I am teaching my granddaughter."

Above: Naa Kahidi Dancers at Sheet'ka Kwaan Naa
   Kahidi Performing Arts Theater.
Above right: Sitka Rose Gallery on Harbor Drive.
Right: Redhot reindeer dogs served by Carol Knuth.

Right page: Crescent Harbor and Sitka Sound.
Above: Islands in Sitka Sound.
Left: New Archangel dancers Julie Schanno, in red, and Kris Wilcox perform Russian folk dance at Harrigan Centennial Hall.

Left: Nelson Frank is one of the many veterans in Southeast Alaska. He was born in Sitka in 1930 and drafted into the Marine Corps in 1950 after graduating from high school. He served six years and was wounded four times fighting in Korea. At the 50th reunion of the 3rd Marines there were only two men left. The only reason the other guy survived was because Nelson carried him out. Nelson came back to Sitka after working with the FAA in Chicago. He says "It was a crazy city for a Sitka boy." He met a nurse in Wisconsin and she followed him home to Sitka. She worked at Mt. Edgecumbe Hospital. "We were married and lived here happily ever after." He is a Haida and Presbyterian elder, and a past president of Sitka's Shee Atiká Incorporated.

Alaskan lynx in the forest of Takshanuk Mountains.

HAINES

Jack Dalton arrived at Haines in 1897 and turned a Tlingit village trading route into a toll road to the Klondike Gold Fields. He was a colorful, gun carrying character who made himself and the Dalton Trail famous. So many gold-hungry people traveled this route that the U.S. Army arrived in Haines in 1903. They established Fort William H. Seward, which remained an active army fort for 20 years. It continued as a military rest camp during World War II, and the Dalton Trail was the route for an evacuation road from Haines to Whitehorse in Canada's Yukon Territory. Part of this road is now the paved Haines Highway, a part of the Alaska Canada Highway system, making Haines and Skagway two of three cities in Southeast Alaska that can be reached by road.

The town of Haines sits 75 miles north of Juneau, up North America's longest and deepest fjord, Lynn Canal, and nestles between the Chilkat and Chilkoot Inlets. Built along the Chilkat Peninsula and at the base of the Takshanuk Mountains, Haines has a picturesque view across two inlets and to the towering Chilkat Mountain Range. With only 53 inches of rain annually, it is a relativity dry area in the Tongass National Forest.

The area around present-day Haines was called "'Dtehshuh" or "End of the Trail" by the Chilkat Tlingit Indians. They carried canoes across the trail used to trade with the interior, saving 20 miles of rowing around the peninsula. Haines was formerly a city but no longer has a municipal government. Voters approved a measure consolidating the City of Haines and Haines Borough into a home rule borough. The area's population is about 1,800.

While the highway links Haines to northern parts of Alaska, western parts of Canada and down to the Lower 48 states, residents still take pride in their independence. Haines doesn't get many cruise ship tourists, which makes the town relaxed and peaceful. Businesses are locally owned and operated. Independent travelers come for the spectacular scenery, abundant wildlife, amazing rivers and gorgeous mountains. Haines has the feel of real Alaska.

Page 75: Haines across Portage Cove.
Left page: Food cache in forest of Takshanuk Mountains.

Above: Haines boat harbor on Portage Cove.

77

STEPHEN KROSCHEL
OWNER, KROSCHEL'S WILDLIFE CENTER

"Haines has it all. It has wilderness. True virgin wilderness. It has old growth forests. And mountains that are just beautiful, ice-covered mountains, even with global warming. The ocean is nearby. The temperatures are quite moderate even in the wintertime. I grew up in Minnesota, yet the winters here in this part of Southeast Alaska are mild in comparison. Lots of lovely snow that is great for snow skiing, snow shoeing, heli-skiing. And the wildlife viewing is unsurpassed."

"I run the Wildlife Center about 27 miles outside of Haines. I love this area. I moved here in June of 2001, and bought a little bit of property. But I was introduced to Haines 25 years ago, doing films for National Geographic and the PBS Series *Wild America*. As a cinematographer I have trained and filmed animals for Disney's Academy Award winning film *Never Cry Wolf*. I have traveled all over Alaska, but nothing captivates me like this area."

"The Wildlife Center covers 60 acres. The part tourists see is a fraction of what we have. There are compounds all over this property. They are all natural settings for film work. Visitors can photograph and video moose, bear, wolves, lynx, porcupine and mink, just to name a few of the many wild animals that live here. This is a place of quietude where they can get close to the animals and see them safely."

"We are trying to give visitors to Haines a unique experience. This is a place where people who hunger desperately to be connected with nature can realize their dreams. Visitors get to see amazing wild creatures in their natural habitat. Many of our visitors may never get this close to Alaskan wildlife like it is here, again in their lifetime. We have people who walk away with tears in their eyes because they've had an intimate experience with our animals. That is what this place is all about. It is not about anything else but getting out a positive message about our natural resources and the wildlife heritage we still have. And we can protect and preserve it, if it is not too late. Alaska is our last frontier and we have a chance. And for us, Haines is the place. I hope to live in Haines for 110 more years."

Left page: Stephen Kroschel and mink.
Above: Porcupine.
Right: Cow moose.

ED LAPEYRI
OWNER, CAPTAIN'S CHOICE MOTEL

"If you really want to see Alaska as it should be, Haines is the place. It is a quiet community. We have lots of wildlife here and lots of roads here. You can get around and do things. It's absolutely a fun area to live in. It's great for kids. It's great for men, and some women. Some women think it is a little remote, you know, but if you love it, you just love it. The women who do stay here love it. They leave and they go Outside but they always end up moving back. People say they will go and retire in Arizona, Florida, but two years later they are back."

"I have lived in Haines since 1970. I have had lots of reasons to leave and I found every excuse to stay. I came up to Haines from California with the timber industry. I worked with a company headquartered out of Portland, Oregon. They operated a mill here in Haines but got out of Alaska in 1976. I didn't want to go down south, so I decided this is where I get off."

"I wanted to stay in Haines because my kids were all small. We have a good school system, little or no drug problems and no crime. I just loved the area. There is so much to do here. Going up the rivers, the fishing is great. It is just a beautiful place to live.

"In the early 1990s they pretty much shut down the Tongass National Forest to the timber industry. About 8,000 people lost their jobs in Southeast Alaska. At that time I had to do something, because I didn't want to leave Haines. I ended up buying a motel. I bought the Captain's Choice in June 1994. It's been 15 years now."

"There has been a real increase in visitors since I bought the motel. There has always been a certain amount of tourism here, but when I was in the timber industry I didn't pay that much attention to it. We get mostly independent travelers in Haines. Several foreign bus tours come through here from Australia, England, France and all over the world. We cater pretty much to these independent travelers. This is the connection to the Alaska Marine Highway and the main highway getting into Alaska, so there are a lot of travelers coming through all the time."

"Visitors find lots of things to see and do here, but I will give you an example about how great it is to live in Haines. You are driving up the highway and get a flat tire. The first car will stop and help you. The first car. You get a flat tire in California and they will run you over."

"The people, the area, the beauty... that's what Haines has to offer. I like to take my boat, go up the river and spend a night or two in a cabin. It's just great. You go up there and it is so quiet. There is something so nice about the sound of quietness. Silence is beautiful sometimes. Everybody has to be somewhere on this planet, and I personally think Haines has got to be in the top five percent of the places in the world to live."

Left: Ed Lapeyri and Bernie at Captain's Choice Motel.
Above: Haines sign at marina.

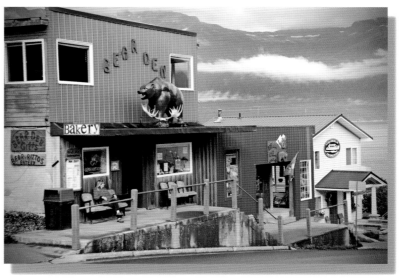

Above: Merrick Bochart, left, and Renee Hoffman work on city mural.
Left: Buildings along Haines Main Street.
Right: Bear Den restaurant and shops.

Eagle soars at Chikat Bald Eagle Preserve

DON "DUCK" HESS
OWNER, CHILKAT RIVER ADVENTURES

"A bear attacked my father on a mountain near Haines in 1965. We had been logging in Sitka and my Dad had come here looking at a timber sale. He put his rifle down and was, what they call, cruising timber. He survived and was able to walk a mile and a half down the mountain, but lost an eye and part of his skull. That brought me to Haines 44 years ago."

"When I was 16 years old, a junior in high school, my Dad wanted to come to Alaska. I was the youngest of four boys and the only one left in school. Dad was going to be 50 years old and thought if he turned 50 he would never make it north. They had a little country store and gas pumps, in Southwestern Oregon. We sold everything and moved to Alaska. I didn't go to school. That summer I got on a fishing boat and had a ball. I met some fine people and made some good money. Meanwhile, my old football coach wrote a letter to the Oregon State Athletic Board and got me eligible for sports. So I went back to Oregon and graduated from high school."

"I immediately returned to Alaska. My folks were in Sitka. I worked in a mill for the summer and in 1958 joined the Air Force. Territory of Alaska is stamped on my records. I was away four years and then returned to Sitka. Dad had gotten a contract logging for Alaska Lumber and Pulp in Sitka. I worked with my brother and Dad for about a year and a half. Then I was the first of the boys to go off on my own. Then Dad's bear attack brought me here to Haines."

"A bear attack sounds like a crazy reason to move to Haines, but the attack brought me here and I got to take a good look around. It is so beautiful here. There is so much that I like about it. Just the raw beauty. I love the Chilkat River. I started running the river in 1966 after buying a flat bottomed homemade river boat with a fifteen horse Chrysler. It's had an attraction for me ever since."

"It was about that time we started the Chilkat River Adventures to share this wilderness with tourists. We patterned the tours after the Rogue River Jet Boats in Southwestern Oregon, although the rivers are totally different. They're shallow water, ours are deep water."

"This is the perfect river for our operation. It has an amazing ecosystem. We see lots of moose, quite a few bears, some wolves, river otter, beaver, porcupine in a tree once-in-a-while, eagle nests, lots of eagles and trumpeter swans. We're 24 miles out of town and have five boats with the capacity for 102 people. We have our own property, which is 48,000 acres right in the middle of the Chilkat Bald Eagle Preserve."

"Haines gives us a small town atmosphere. My wife and I were both raised in small towns. We go south in the winter some, but that just makes us love it here more. When you get down in the highway traffic, oh God, I hate it! Up here we get upset if there are two cars in front of us at a stop sign. Haines is the real Alaska."

Cruise West's *Spirit of Columbia* at Port Chilkoot Dock on Portage Cove near Haines.

Crystal Cruises ship docked at Skagway port beyond White Pass & Yukon Route passenger rail cars. Parsons Peak is in the background.

SKAGWAY

Skagway and the nearby ghost town of Dyea were the starting points for more than 40,000 Gold Rush stampeders in 1897. They gathered in these frontier cities to make their way over the treacherous Chilkoot Trail into Yukon gold fields. It was called Skagua by the local Tlingit Natives which means "Windy Place with White Caps on the Water." During the balmy summers there are very few white caps and little wind.

An Irishman named Michael Heney talked a group of Englishmen into financing the construction of a railroad that ran over the White Pass Trail to Whitehorse in Canada's Yukon. It was an amazing feat of construction which kept Skagway going economically when the Gold Rush ended. Today the railroad is one of the most popular tourist attractions in Alaska.

Located at the end of the Taiya Inlet, Skagway is the reincarnated version of the Klondike Gold Rush days. The city has captured the past and takes great pride in sharing it on a daily basis with thousands of eager visitors who step off cruise ships and onto her wooden sidewalks every summer. Populated by less than 1,000 people, the city seems to burst at the seams when visitors arrive.

Looking like a stage set, the entire town has survived intact much as it was more than 100 years in the past. Today it's all part of the Klondike Gold Rush National Historical Park which takes in Skagway, the Chilkoot Trail, The White Pass Trail corridor and a Seattle visitor center. Visitors often recognize the area as a backdrop for Jack London's book, *The Call of the Wild*.

While Skagway takes some criticism for being too tourist oriented, the crowded streets and busy vendors are reminiscent of the early days. It is vibrant, colorful and very much alive. The old wooden buildings are painted in their original colors and well preserved in the relatively dry climate. Many locals dress in gold rush era costumes, as the train comes and goes in a cloud of steam and excitement. Skagway has always been an exciting town.

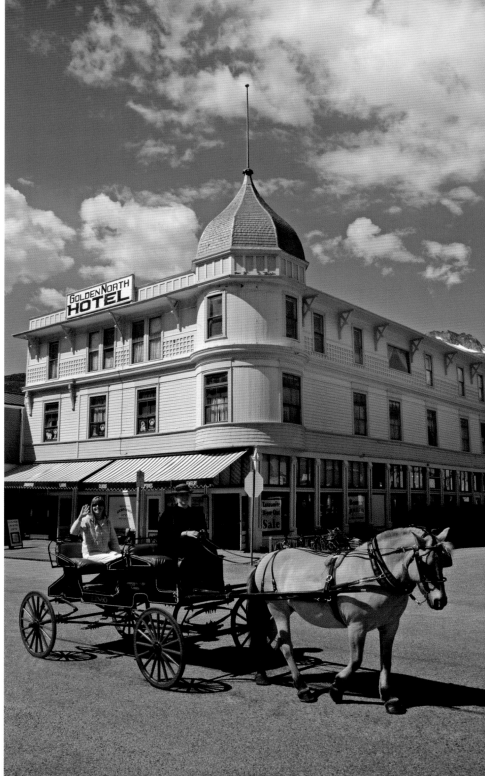

Page 85: Street car tours on Broadway,
   the main street of Skagway.
Left page: Princess cruise ship docked at the Port
   of Skagway. Taiya Inlet is in the background.
Above: The Klondike Highway leads to points
   north from Skagway.
Right: Pamela Dockter tours a visitor around the
   sights of Skagway.

STEVE HITES
OWNER, SKAGWAY STREET CAR COMPANY

"I believe there is an echo set off by events and sometimes you can hear it. I am not talking about metaphysical mumbo jumbo, I am talking about the human ability to sense and feel events that have gone before us. You can feel it when you stand in Pompeii. You can feel it when you stand in front of the capitol building in Washington D.C., and you can feel it when you are on a lonely prairie looking across to the west, imagining Lewis and Clark aside their keel boat wondering what's ahead."

"In Skagway that echo is extremely easy to hear; the focus is so absolute. There was one single event that happened. Like a thunderclap, it was the Klondike Stampede. That echo has reverberated through the decades and into a second century. If you stop in the evening when the cruise ships are gone, you can hear it in the wind. If you step out on Broadway, right at noon, as the train arrives and the ships are here and there are 15,000 people in this valley, you can hear it. Put your ear out and it's the sound of straining horses and barking dogs and yelling men and the sounds of honky-tonk

pianos in this explosion that happens. We get to recreate that here every day, all summer long. We create that explosion over and over and over. The Klondike Gold Rush is part of the American story, and this particular venue is where we will continue to tell that story as long as the American flag shall fly. As long as there is a country, Skagway will continue to interpret that amazing, singular event, the Klondike Gold Rush, forever."

"Skagway is unique; it never burned. Individual buildings were lost to fire, but no major fire burned down the whole commercial district. Juneau burned once, Fairbanks burned twice, Nome burned three times and Atlin, British Columbia burned down five times. Of all the gold rush towns in the north, only Skagway survived intact, including hotels, saloons and freighting companies. From the turn of the century to the present era, historians have recognized the uniqueness of the architectural fabric and a historical district has been created where those things are protected."

"I grew up in Colorado, surrounded by abandoned mines and little narrow gauge railroads. I was fascinated by old stories of building tall wooden trestles that arched across deep chasms. I wanted to work on the prettiest railroad you could find under the American flag, and learned there were two in Alaska. By chance my mother was planning a trip and I went with her to the travel agency. They had a brochure showing a narrow gauge train going along a blue lake, with tall mountains and glaciers and it said, 'Come North Where The World Is Young.' It was from the White Pass & Yukon Route in Skagway, Alaska. I announced to my parents I was going away to work on that railroad. My mom said I couldn't even wash my own socks. But that didn't stop me."

"As I was leaving for Alaska, my mom asked that on my way to the ferry terminal in Seattle, I visit Whitworth College, where I had been accepted. She gave me a check for the first semester, just in case it worked out. It was a cute school, so I asked where I would stay and was taken to one of the dorms. I was introduced to another freshman, Dean Warner. He told me he was from Skagway, Alaska. I was shocked. That was where I was going to work on the railroad, I told him. He said they weren't hiring up there until spring, and then we could both go up and work for the railroad. I stayed at the college and spent most of the winter researching Skagway. One book, *Scenic and Historic Views in Skagway, Alaska 1933: A Tour Onboard the Skagway Street Car*, by Martin Itchen changed my life."

"With the wind howling and the snow blowing sideways, Dean brought me home to Skagway in December 1972. As we drove the empty street into town, I looked over and saw deserted container flats from a narrow gauge railroad and thought, 'My God, it's 1958 in Colorado. I am home.' Thirty-seven years later I am still in Skagway."

Engine Number 69 of the White Pass & Yukon Route has been in service since 1908.

CARLIN "BUCKWHEAT" DONAHUE
EXECUTIVE DIRECTOR,
SKAGWAY CONVENTION
& VISITORS BUREAU

"I was traveling on the Alaska Marine Highway System in 1981 on the motor vessel *Columbia* and had too much to drink, passed out and slept through Juneau. When I woke up I got off in Skagway. I felt strangely comfortable here. Alaska got into my soul and this was the place for me."

"Something about Skagway got under my skin. Crawling off the ferry I met a girl and stayed with her for the Fourth of July weekend. I won the watermelon-spitting contest! I thought that was great. I had never even heard of these things growing up in Denver. They just don't have things like the egg toss. Now I have organized the most participants in an egg-tossing contest. We whipped up on Wrangell, yes indeed. 1,162 people tossed eggs in Skagway, beating Wrangell's record of 382. It's this kind of small town fun that's so great."

"The people make this place special. It's a confidence that people here feel. Remember when we were kids, our parents said in America you can grow up and be President. That gave me confidence that I could do whatever I wanted. That same spirit is everywhere in Alaska. I like being around people who, when they decide to do something, they go out and do it. I wasn't finding people like that in Denver. I don't feel there are walls here that delineate the classes of society prevalent in other places. This is one of the main attractions of Alaska. Confident people everywhere. In a manner far exceeding levels that you find in other places."

"The Skagway community is very tight knit. I know this from personal experiences. Back in 1997 my house burned and I had to rebuild. I started in January, not the best time of the year. I'm at the house cleaning and taking trash out. A couple of guys who heard about my bad luck showed up with their tool belts to help. By 7:30 am there were 100 people helping. For the next two days the house was torn down and we were having all kinds of fun. All this help was given voluntarily. I knew who all of them were, but I had never had a beer with them. This is just one example of the generosity of the people here."

"Skagway also has the land. We are a busy destination port. Yet you get 10 feet off the road and welcome to the bush. I can hike to the top of a mountain, look off in any direction and see uninterrupted wilderness. It goes on forever and ever. Even though you know there are little towns and villages out there, they don't bug you. They're of such little consequence that they don't bother you because the wilderness is that big."

"And the history of Skagway is so rich. You have people like Robert Service and Jack London who help bring the rest of us up to speed about Alaska and the Yukon. Their words still echo and reverberate across the territory today. I love reading about it and being able to go back 110 years ago when Jack London actually hiked the Chilkoot Trail into the Yukon, and down the river to Nome. He did all those things."

"I have been a guide and an actor on the Skagway stage. I have performed Robert Service poetry onboard cruise ships. I have been at my present job, executive director of the Skagway Convention & Visitors Bureau, for 10 years. I didn't know what I would do in Skagway, which was part of the attraction. I just came because it felt like it was what I was supposed to do. I am glad I did. I bought a grave here. This is where I will stay."

Above: Christina Byron-Silvoso and Tom Martin
  re-enact the days of Soapy Smith, a con artist and
  gangster who ran the city in the late 1890s.
Right: In costumes of the Gold Rush Days, Meredith
  Hinckley, left, and Sara Waisanen wait for customers
  outside the famous Red Onion Saloon.

JOHN & JAN TRONRUD
OWNERS, THE WHITE HOUSE BED & BREAKFAST

"We are a typical Skagway story. Young people who came to work for the summer, fell in love and decided to stay. Skagway has always been friendly. Everybody seems to know everybody and they make you feel like family. The scenery is beautiful, the mountains come out of the water and it has clear skies. The Fourth of July is when you see former residents. It's old home week. Even if people leave, Skagway has a tie that keeps you connected."

"I came to Skagway in 1973. After a couple of college quarters, I came back for good. Salt Lake isn't a big city, but the traffic, smog and getting robbed at gunpoint made me want to leave," John said. "I was a night clerk in a 24-hour grocery store. I could see the bullets in the cylinder. I thought, Skagway was a rough town, but I'm going back."

"My brother got me a summer job with the White Pass railroad. Why spend years in college, when I made a good living and Skagway was a nice town? That's how I ended up here. I've been working on the waterfront ever since. It's a little small if you're single and a little isolated, but since we built the highway a lot of things make it a great place to live."

"The Westmark offered me a job as their front desk manager in Skagway for the summer, after finishing my hotel degree," Jan recalled. "John and I met and started dating in July. When September rolled around, I decided to stay. That was 1989. We just had our 20th wedding anniversary."

"We bought The White House Bed & Breakfast with my brother and his

wife in 1990," John remembers. "It was damaged in a fire years earlier. My brother and I helped fight that fire. It was cold, in the middle of winter and the wind was howling. Everyone comes out for fires. We were amazed we put it out. Later, the owners were getting older. They talked about rebuilding, but the husband passed away and we knew the rebuild plans would not become reality. Laurie, my brother's wife, was a friend of the family and she asked about buying it. The woman said yes."

"The White House was a perfect fit for us. Laurie was working at the bank at that time, so she had a banking background. Both of the guys had built their own homes. I had the hotel experience," Jan said. "We bought the place, fixed it up and opened to guests in 1997."

"We like the mix of interesting visitors with a small, tight knit community that feels like family. There are stories that just go on and on about people who step up to the plate when the chips are down for their neighbors. It's really remarkable. The community rallies to fundraise for families having financial difficulties or medical challenges. You see the difference it makes in people's lives when the community comes together."

"Another unique thing about Skagway, and life-giving for the residents, is that in four minutes we can be hiking in the forest. It doesn't matter if there are tons of people in town, it gives you an instant feeling of relief. Today I was out fishing right alongside a humpback whale. I was taking pictures of him all day. We were both fishing and passing within 100 feet of each other. National Geographic is in our backyard."

Buildings in Skagway are painted in colors used during the gold rush era.

"Newsies" Sunnie Cotton, left, and Jade Cook give visitors the gold rush era *Skaguay Alaskan* newspaper.

Tourists can cruise the town in classic rental cars like this rare 1955 Ford Crown Victoria.

A brown bear moves along a creek in Yakutat.

YAKUTAT

The sign at the Yakutat Lodge just across from the airport terminal says it best: "Food, Shelter, Booze." Welcome to Yakutat! The northern-most town in Southeast Alaska, Yakutat is full of surprises. They start with long sandy beaches, framed by stacks of driftwood that seem to go on forever. And there's surfing. That's right. Yakutat is quickly becoming popular with surfers around the world.

The Yakutat area is blessed by nature. Within a 15 minute sightseeing flight is the huge Russell Fjord Wilderness Area, Mount Saint Elias and its sister peaks tower in the distance, rising from Yakutat Bay. World War II relics rust in lush green rainforests, and icebergs float from Yakutat Glacier into dazzling Harlequin Lake. Adding to the grandeur is magnificent Hubbard Glacier, the world's largest tidewater glacier, less than 30 miles away. The local streams teem with fish, salmon almost jump into fishing boats, majestic brown bears stroll confidently within sight and eagles soar above.

The town itself is also a surprise. Yakutat City is the largest incorporated area in the United States. Covering a total area of 9,459 square miles, it's larger than two or three smaller states. This huge area has a population of less than 800 people. The real shock is there isn't a town. They do have a post office on the main airport road, a combination gas station store on one dirt road, a state trooper office down another, and a host of fishing and hunting lodges scattered in the surrounding forests. There's also a nice marina. But no town. It's old style Alaska. And the locals want to keep it that way. The local Chamber of Commerce has plans to create a visitor's center, refurbishing an old cannery by the waterfront. The local Native association plans to give performances. There's also an interesting surf shop in one of the small neighborhoods. A number of fine artists call Yakutat home. The area is special. What is no surprise is that anyone with a love for natural rugged beauty and an adventurous spirit will love Yakutat.

Page 95: Commercial fishing boat travels the waters
  of Yakutat Bay with Mount Saint Elias in the background.
Left page: Dangerous River Bridge at Harlequin Lake with
  icebergs fed from Yakutat Glacier.

Above: Charter captain Scott Chadwick shows his halibut at
  Yakutat Boat Harbor, with his boat the *Sea Wolf* moored behind.

WALTER PORTER
COMMUNITY LEADER

"I care deeply about the development of our beautiful area and have been elected president of the Yakutat Chamber of Commerce. I am also a Tlingit elder born in Yakutat in 1944, just before WWII was over. I lived here until 1956 when I went to Haines to finish school. Then I traveled for about 10 years. I came back here when my mother passed away in 1972. My wife and I met at a friend's wedding in the spring and we got married in September that same year. While we lived and worked outside of here for a number of years, Yakutat has always been home to us."

"This is a large sport fishing community and we appreciate the visiting fishermen greatly. We also want to attract more tourist activity so the entire community can benefit from visitors. There are a lot of things here for tourists."

"Yakutat has the Hubbard Glacier. Even though many ships have gone there, it is still relatively unknown. The glacier is 700 feet high and seven miles across. It is just gigantic. It is the most active of all the glaciers in Alaska. They call it the Galloping Glacier. It did get famous in the mid-1980s, when it bumped up against a mountain and flooded the whole fjord. It broke away in time so that it did not flood over into Yakutat."

"Yakutat is also a cultural destination. We have a number of talented artists, dancers and cultural educators. We can teach visitors about our native language, mythology and history with interactive presentations. We also want to teach our ancient art of imagining. Through our storytelling history we were taught to imagine our past."

"Yakutat has incredible natural beauty. We take visitors up to the glacier with small boat charter sightseeing operations, teach them how to say the different Tlingit names of animals, like the killer whale, seal and bear. We encourage the cultural seeker. A man by the name of Ted Valley tells wonderful stories. When he was a young boy they would canoe up to the glacier. When the bow of the boat touched the land, the elder would speak to the country and apologize for bothering the spirits there. He would explain what they were doing, what they would do with the things they took and how long they were going to stay. It is fabulous."

"Our ancient stories resonate with everyone, not just Native people. It's just like the stars for guidance, everyone in the world knows that. It's like asking how a baby communicates. How did a baby communicate a million years ago? How about a million years from now. They cry. It is like truth. It never changes. You and I change, but truth itself is always the same. There is only one truth. The Yakutat area resonates in such a way it is a special place we can share with each other. It has its own power, its own spirit, and we learn from it."

Above: Gill net fisherman Mark Donahue
catches salmon from the Lower Situk River.
Right: Fisherman's hut along river's edge.

99

JACK ENDICOTT
OWNER, ICY WAVES SURF SHOP

"Yakutat is a cool place. It's a neat little town, just a beautiful little town. When it's clear and nice, it is unbeatable. On the other hand, when it's raining an inch a day for weeks on end and blowing, you think, 'Why am I here?' But one day afterwards when the sun pops out and Mt. St. Elias shines, you think, 'Wow! I've been here for 30 years now, and when I go out in the bay the mountains still bring tears to my eyes.'"

"We had been taking our kids to Hawaii for several years. After one trip they said the surfing waves are just as good in Yakutat. All we need are some wetsuits, surfboards and stuff. My wife suggested using our tax refund to see what could be done. So we bought wetsuits and surfboards. My wife's sister, a graphic artist, came up with some designs for us. We tried all kinds of names. Then my wife Laura, thinking of the waters here, said it should be called Icy Waves. So away we went..."

"We ordered 300 t-shirts with the new name. I will never forget it. I thought we would be giving t-shirts away for birthdays, anniversaries and would have t-shirts forever. Then they started selling. A lot. A reporter for the Juneau Weekly did an article on us. Then the Juneau Empire ran a little article. AP wire picked it up and it went nation wide. Then I will never forget, a guy called and said my name is so and so with CBS News, we would like to do a news segment on your surf shop for the evening news. They spent three days interviewing people and taking all kinds of surfing pictures. Their little two minute segment got a huge response. We got bushels of mail and e-mails. It was crazy. It was awesome."

All of a sudden the big pro surfers and board makers started calling. Last Thanksgiving the Red Bull Team came and they caught some incredibly big waves. There were almost more photographers than there were surfers. There were surfers from Brazil, Tahiti, Australia and Hawaii. It was amazing."

"I love the family atmosphere in Yakutat, the safety and the security. If you break down along the road, the next person is going to help you. It's comforting, very comforting. You do not have to lock your doors or take the keys out of your car. If anyone gets injured or hurt, the whole town helps. No one ever goes hungry here. Ever. It's a great place to raise kids. You know that no one is going to abduct your kids. Your neighbors are watching your kids. The kids have to be pretty straight and narrow."

"I've lived in Yakutat since 1980. My job brought me here. I work for the National Weather Service. I started my career in Kodiak, Alaska, moved to Cold Bay for a couple of years and then to Juneau. Then I was sent to Salt Lake City and from there to Nebraska. I bid Yakutat in 1980 and fell in love with it. Thirty years later we still love it."

Surfer David Brown and flat waters of Monti Bay.

Above: Called Graveyard Beach by locals, the area is
popular with tourists and surfers alike.
Right: Footprints lead across the sand to the waters
of Yakutat Bay, with the Wrangell-Saint Elias
Mountain Range in the distance.

Top: Fishing boat with Wrangell-St. Elias Range.
Left: Yakutat Cold Storage dock on Monti Bay.

Right: Dean Kozlowski from Chicago holds his 20 lb. silver salmon.
Facing page: Boat heads to Leonard's Landing Lodge on Yakutat Bay.

Hubbard Glacier calves into Disenchantment Bay at Gilbert Point.

HUBBARD GLACIER

Flowing from the Saint Elias Mountains into Disenchantment Bay, part of the 545 square mile Russell Fjord Wilderness Area, is the striking Hubbard Glacier. It was named after Gardiner Hubbard, a Regent of the Smithsonian Institution and first president of the National Geographic Society. Stretching 76 miles to the sea, this is the longest tidewater glacier in the world and is Alaska's most active, earning the nickname "Galloping Glacier."

In the spring of 1986 it "galloped" across the channel and dammed off the mouth of Russell Fjord. The move brought world attention to the Hubbard Glacier and volunteers flocked to Yakutat, only 30 miles south of the glacier, to rescue trapped marine animals. When the summer melt came the waters behind the dammed channel rose quickly. The water pressure finally broke though the glacier wall in October. The glacier eventually receded, but galloped to block the channel again in 2002. This blockage lasted only a short time. Again in 2008 the glacier surged to within a couple hundred yards of damming the channel.

This is a visually magnificent area, but what makes it so special and exciting is the activity of Hubbard Glacier. It routinely calves at high tide releasing pieces of ice as tall as a 10-story building. Strong currents and riptides flow between the face of the glacier and Gilbert Point. It is very dramatic to observe. The glacier groans, cracks and explodes in sound, sight and color, as the huge masses of ice break free from this towering blue icy wall and throw gallons of bay water into the sky. Beautifully framed by majestic mountains, Hubbard Glacier is a remarkable sight to see.

Page 105: Glacier ice crashes into the waters
   of Disenchantment Bay.
Left page: Icebergs float across the waters of
   Disenchantment Bay with the Saint Elias Mountain
   Range behind.
Above: Walls of ice thunder into the water from
   Hubbard Glacier's huge face.
Right: An Alaskan grey seal with a salmon.

An Alaska Airlines Boeing 737-400 takes off from the Wrangell Airport. The airline is the primary means of transportation between Southeastern Alaska cities and the Lower 48 states.

Right: Wrangell Saint Elias Range

Wings of Alaska Cessna Grand Caravan taking off at Juneau International Airport.

THANK YOU !

Many "Friends of *Southeast Alaska*" helped in the creation of this book. Flip Todd of Todd Communications had the vision to make an idea into a reality. We thank all the characters for spending time with us, so their words could add a human touch to these pages. A special thank you to the organizations and people who made it possible to photograph and write about the many wonderful parts of Southeast Alaska. They include:

Alaska Airlines: Greg & Lisa Latimer, Bill McKay, Susan Bramstedt
Holland America Line: Judy Palmer, Erik Elvejord
Wings of Alaska: Carl Ramsa

Ketchikan:	Dragon London, Ketchikan Convention & Visitors Bureau
	Saxman Native Village & Totem Park
Wrangell:	Carol Rushmore, City & Borough of Wrangell
	Alaskan Sourdough Lodge
Petersburg:	Jim Johnson
	Patti Wagon Tours

Juneau:	Elizabeth Arnett, Juneau Convention & Visitors Bureau
	Rich and Peggy Poor
	Dr. Andy & Mae Moosa
Hoonah:	Ozzie Sheakley, Tlingit Elder
	Tyler Hickman, Icy Strait Point
	Don Rosenberger, Icy Strait Point
Sitka:	Totem Square Inn
Haines:	Captain's Choice Motel
	Lori Stepansky, Haines Convention & Visitor Bureau
Skagway:	Gary Danielson, White Pass & Yukon Route
	Skagway Convention & Visitors Bureau
	The White House Bed & Breakfast
Yakutat:	Reggie Krkovich, Yakutat Inn
	Norm Isrealson
Seattle:	Captain Charles & Faye Davis
	Danna Siverts
	Clark Emery
	Natalie Luke

Totem in Saxman Native Village and Totem Park, Ketchikan.
Back cover: Rafting on Mendenhall River, McGinnis Mountain
   to left and Mt. Stroller White, near Juneau.